First Facts®

Amazing Animal Architects

AMAZING
Animal Architects
Underground

A 4D BOOK

by Rebecca Rissman

Consultants:
James L. Gould
Professor
Department of Ecology and Evolutionary Biology
Princeton University

Carol Grant Gould
Science Writer
Princeton, N.J.

PEBBLE
a capstone imprint

Download the Capstone 4D app!

- Ask an adult to download the Capstone 4D app.
- Scan the cover and stars inside the book for additional content.

When you scan a spread, you'll find fun extra stuff to go with this book! You can also find these things on the web at www.capstone4D.com using the password: underground.26813

First Facts are published by Pebble
1710 Roe Crest Drive, North Mankato, Minnesota 56003
www.mycapstone.com

Library of Congress Cataloging-in-Publication Data
Names: Rissman, Rebecca, author.
Title: Amazing animal architects underground : A 4D book / by
  Rebecca Rissman.
Description: North Mankato, Minnesota : an imprint of Pebble, [2019] |
  Series: First facts. Amazing animal architects | Audience: Ages 6–8. |
  Includes index.
Identifiers: LCCN 2017057831 (print) | LCCN 2018000325 (ebook) | ISBN
  9781543526899 (ebook PDF) | ISBN 9781543526813 (hardcover) | ISBN
  9781543526851 (pbk.)
Subjects: LCSH: Burrowing animals—Juvenile literature. |
  Animals—Habitations—Juvenile literature. | Animal behavior—Juvenile
  literature.
Classification: LCC QL756.15 (ebook) | LCC QL756.15 .R57 2018 (print) | DDC
  591.56/48—dc23
LC record available at https://lccn.loc.gov/2017057831

Editorial Credits
Karen Aleo, editor; Sarah Bennett, designer; Morgan Walters, media researcher;
Tori Abraham, production specialist

Photo Credits
Getty Images: David Tipling, 19, TOM MCHUGH, 7; Newscom: H. Schmidbauer/picture alliance/blickwinkel/H, 21, Laurie Campbell/NHPA/Photoshot, 15; Shutterstock: Chutima Chaochaiya, (blueprint) design element, Miloje, (grunge) design element, Natalia5988, (brush grunge) design element, Nicole S Glass, 5, Peter Hermes Furian, (map) design element, Pong Wira, 11, Salparadis, 9, sauletas, 17, Sokolov Alexey, Cover, Zoltan Tarlacz, 13

Printed in China.
000306

Table of Contents

An Underground Construction Zone

Some of the most amazing underground homes aren't built by humans. They are built by animals. These animals scratch, chew, and scrape. They dig and make **burrows**. They make complex underground homes. The homes protect some animals from **predators**. They're also good places to store food and raise young.

burrow—a hole or tunnel used as a house

predator—an animal that hunts other animals for food

A prairie dog digs its underground home.

Pocket Gophers

Pocket gophers dig down into the soil. These small animals dig with strong front legs, sharp claws, and long teeth.

Pocket gophers make **shallow** tunnels. They crawl through them and eat plant roots. The gophers dig deep tunnels too. They make chambers for storing food, sleeping, and raising young. These chambers keep them safe from predators.

shallow—not deep

Gophers burrow below the ground. The entrance is often marked by a small, fan-shaped pile of soil.

FACT

Gophers can close their lips around their long teeth. This keeps dirt out of their mouths when they dig with their teeth.

Leaf-Cutter Ants

Leaf-cutter ants dig tunnels and chambers that stretch deep into the ground. The ants use them to raise young. But that's not all.

The ants are skilled gardeners. They bring pieces of leaves to the nest. They use the leaves to grow a **fungus**. Then the ants eat the fungus.

fungus—a living thing similar to a plant, but without flowers, leaves, or green coloring; fungi are a group of organisms that include mushrooms.

WHERE LEAF-CUTTER ANTS LIVE

Leaf-cutter ants build their nests in the rain forests.

Trapdoor Spiders

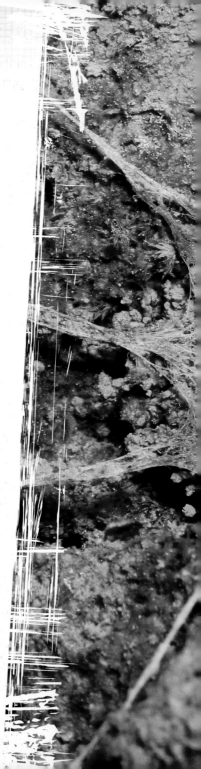

A spider waits in its hidden burrow. A cricket comes close. The spider bursts through a trapdoor. It drags the **prey** inside to eat it.

Trapdoor spiders make underground burrows. They line their burrows with silk, **saliva**, and soil. Most trapdoor spiders make a door for the burrow opening. The trapdoor swings on a **hinge** and is **camouflaged**. This makes the burrow hard to see.

prey—an animal hunted by another animal for food
saliva—the liquid in the mouth
hinge—a moveable part where two things are connected
camouflage—to be made to blend in with the things around it

WHERE TRAPDOOR SPIDERS LIVE

Trapdoor spiders burrow in warm grassy areas, hillsides, or riverbanks.

RANGE MAP

FACT

Some types of trapdoor spiders use strings of silk to tell them when prey is near. When the prey touches the silk, the spider feels the string move. It rushes out to catch the prey.

Prairie Dogs

Many prairie dogs live in big groups called towns. They work together to dig underground homes. They use their strong paws and sharp claws to dig tunnels, chambers, and openings. Some chambers are used for raising young. Others are used for sleeping or storing waste.

Prairie dogs aren't the only ones using their burrows. Ferrets and other small animals sometimes crawl in too.

FACT

A 25,000-square mile (64,750-square kilometer) prairie dog town was once discovered in Texas. About 400 million prairie dogs lived there.

WHERE PRAIRIE DOGS LIVE

Prairie dog towns can be found in open grasslands. A mound of packed soil is often at the burrow entrance.

RANGE MAP

European Badgers

European badgers dig homes called setts. They use their strong legs and long claws to scrape away at the soil. The badgers make tunnels and chambers. They often dig many entrance holes.

The badgers keep their setts clean. They use special chambers for waste. They sleep on grass and leaves. The badgers often replace this bedding to keep it fresh.

WHERE EUROPEAN BADGERS LIVE

A European badger sett is often on the slope of a hill.

Eastern Moles

Dig, dig, dig. A mole is at work! Eastern moles mostly live below the ground. They have wide front paws and sharp claws. They use them to dig shallow, twisting tunnels. This is where they find insects to eat. They also dig deeper tunnels that lead to chambers. The moles use these areas to rest, store food, and raise young.

WHERE EASTERN MOLES LIVE

As moles dig, they push the extra dirt out of their tunnels onto the surface. These form small mounds called molehills.

RANGE MAP

FACT

Moles and gophers are sometimes confused for the other. But a mole has a long snout and tiny eyes. Gophers have shorter snouts and long front teeth.

European Water Voles

A European water vole jumps into the water. It then slips into an underwater tunnel.

Water voles use their sharp teeth and claws to make burrows near rivers. The burrows can have entrances below, at, or above the water. The voles dig chambers for food **storage**, resting, and raising young. To stay dry, these chambers are higher than the water.

storage—a place to save things or to put things away

WHERE EUROPEAN WATER VOLES LIVE

Water voles dig oval-shaped holes close to rivers.

Naked Mole-Rats

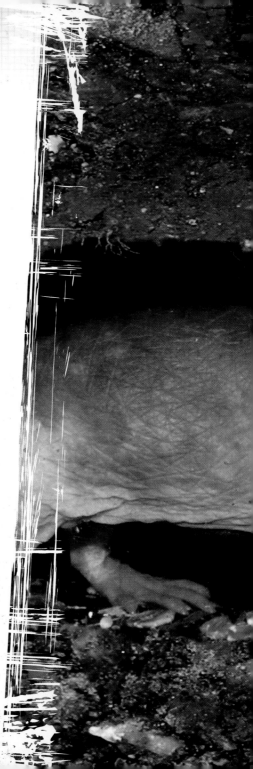

What expert digger is mostly hairless? A naked mole-rat!

These rodents live in **colonies**. They work together to dig tunnels and chambers. Chambers are used for newborn pups, for waste, and for food storage. The tunnels keep the mole-rats safe from harsh **temperatures** outside.

colony—a large group of animals or creatures that live together in the same area

temperature—the measure of how hot or cold something is

WHERE NAKED MOLE-RATS LIVE

Naked mole-rats make small molehills. The hills are shaped like volcanoes.

RANGE MAP

FACT

Naked mole-rat colonies can be very large. Their tunnel systems can cover an area the size of six football fields.

Glossary

burrow (BUHR-oh)—a hole or tunnel used as a house

camouflage (KA-muh-flahzh)—to be made to blend in with the things around it

colony (KAH-luh-nee)—a large group of animals or creatures that live together in the same area

fungus (FUHN-guhs)—a living thing similar to a plant, but without flowers, leaves, or green coloring; fungi are a group of organisms that include mushrooms.

hinge (HINJ)—a moveable part where two things are connected; a door swings open on a hinge.

predator (PRED-uh-tur)—an animal that hunts other animals for food

prey (PRAY)—an animal hunted by another animal for food

saliva (suh-LYE-vuh)—the liquid in the mouth

shallow (SHAL-oh)—not deep

storage (STOR-ij)—a place to save things or to put things away

temperature (TEM-pur-uh-chur)—the measure of how hot or cold something is

Read More

Phillips, Dee. *Badger's Burrow.* The Hole Truth!: Underground Animal Life. New York: Bearport Publishing, 2013.

Rustad, Martha E. H. *Baby Animals in Burrows.* Baby Animals and Their Homes. North Mankato, Minn.: Capstone Press, 2017.

Spilsbury, Richard. *Burrow.* Look Inside. Chicago: Heinemann Library, 2013.

Internet Sites

Use FactHound to find Internet sites related to this book.

Visit *www.facthound.com*

Just type in 9781543526813 and go.

Super-cool stuff! Check out projects, games, and lots more at **www.capstonekids.com**

Critical Thinking Questions

1. Some animals build underground homes with many separate rooms or chambers. How do they use these spaces?

2. What are some body parts that help animals dig?

3. How are a mole and pocket gopher the same? How are they different?

Index

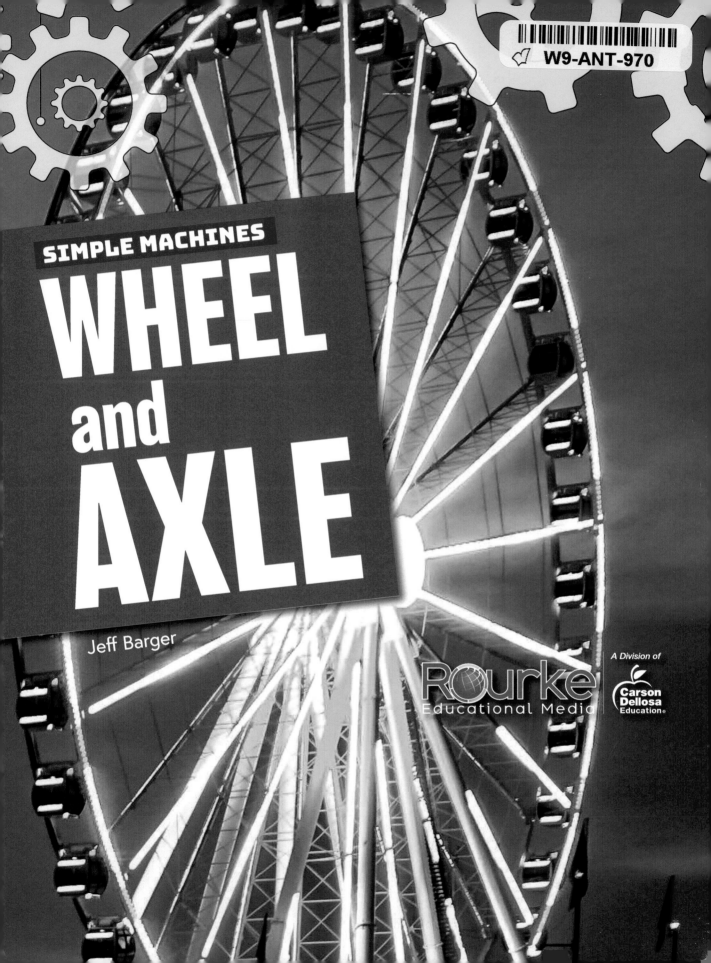

SIMPLE MACHINES

WHEEL and AXLE

Jeff Barger

A Division of

ROurke
Educational Media

Carson
Dellosa
Education

Before, During, and After Reading Activities

Before Reading: Building Background Knowledge and Academic Vocabulary

"Before Reading" strategies activate prior knowledge and set a purpose for reading. Before reading a book, it is important to tap into what your child or students already know about the topic. This will help them develop their vocabulary and increase their reading comprehension.

Questions and activities to build background knowledge:
1. *Look at the cover of the book. What will this book be about?*
2. *What do you already know about the topic?*
3. *Let's study the Table of Contents. What will you learn about in the book's chapters?*
4. *What would you like to learn about this topic? Do you think you might learn about it from this book? Why or why not?*

Building Academic Vocabulary

Building academic vocabulary is critical to understanding subject content.
Assist your child or students to gain meaning of the following vocabulary words.
Content Area Vocabulary
Read the list. What do these words mean?

- *axle*
- *complex*
- *effort*
- *force*
- *friction*
- *tiller*

During Reading: Writing Component

"During Reading" strategies help to make connections, monitor understanding, generate questions, and stay focused.
1. *While reading, write in your reading journal any questions you have or anything you do not understand.*
2. *After completing each chapter, write a summary of the chapter in your reading journal.*
3. *While reading, make connections with the text and write them in your reading journal.*
   a) Text to Self – What does this remind me of in my life? What were my feelings when I read this?
   b) Text to Text – What does this remind me of in another book I've read? How is this different from other books I've read?
   c) Text to World – What does this remind me of in the real world? Have I heard about this before? (News, current events, school, etc.…)

After Reading: Comprehension and Extension Activity

"After Reading" strategies provide an opportunity to summarize, question, reflect, discuss, and respond to text. After reading the book, work on the following questions with your child or students to check their level of reading comprehension and content mastery.
1. *How do wheels make work take less effort? (Summarize)*
2. *Why do we need wheels? (Infer)*
3. *What are two items at school that have wheels? (Asking Questions)*
4. *Name one way you have used wheels today. (Text-to-Self Connection)*

Extension Activity
During your day, look for different items that use wheels. See if you can count ten different items. Look on your way to school. Can you find items in your classroom or local library? What items use wheels at home? As you list the items, consider the different sizes of the wheels as well. Think about why items have different wheel sizes.

TABLE OF CONTENTS

Machines at the Store

Walk into a grocery store. You see rows of food. What else is there? Machines are all around. Refrigerators cool slices of cheese. Freezers keep ice cream frozen. A machine mists leafy vegetables.

A clerk scans a box. The price appears on a machine. It is time to pay. A card reader allows you to pay. All of these are **complex** machines. They have several moving parts.

A scanner reads a code on an item. It sends information to the register. The scanner and register are complex machines.

Other machines at the store are simple. They do not have many parts. Do you lift a cart into the store? No, a ramp allows carts to move up. It is an inclined plane. An inclined plane is a simple machine. Simple machines make work easier.

There are six simple machines. They are the wheel and axle, inclined plane, lever, pulley, screw, and wedge.

inclined plane

Machines are on water bottles. The cap is a screw. It keeps water inside the bottle. A tab on a can is a lever. Bubble gum slides down an inclined plane.

What Are Wheels?

There are many wheels at the store. Grocery carts have four wheels. Cars parked outside have wheels. Pasta can come in a wheel shape. So how do these wheels do work?

axle

Another name for a rod is a shaft. A rod by itself does not move, or stays rigid.

A wheel needs an **axle**. This rod connects wheels. The axle is in the center of the wheel. It allows the wheel to turn. Look under a skateboard. You see the axle connecting the wheels.

Wheels Doing Work

All machines help you use less **effort**. Think back to the grocery store. Imagine a cart without wheels. You pull it down the aisle. You push it to check out. Shopping would be harder without wheels.

Simple machines give us mechanical advantage. This means less effort to do the same work. Do wheels on the cart change your grocery list? You still have to shop. With wheels, it is much easier.

Grocery items come in boxes. Carts help workers carry the boxes to the shelves. This means less effort for them.

Why do wheels work? They reduce **friction**. Rubbing of two objects creates friction. This makes moving slower. Drag your feet instead of walking. Do you move slower or faster?

Rub your hands together. The heat you feel comes from friction.

Library carts are heavy. Without wheels, you would have to pull the cart. Think of the friction. The noise would not make your librarian happy.

Wheels in the Yard

Do you want to grow a garden? Wheels can help! You will need soil. A bag of soil is heavy. Take a load off. Put it in a wheelbarrow. Load several bags into the wheelbarrow. Its wheel and axle will move it along.

A **tiller** prepares the soil for planting. It uses steel wheels to loosen the soil.

Wheels help with other outside jobs. Spreaders are buckets that travel on wheels. A second wheel is under the bucket. Seed lands on this wheel. The wheel spins. This spreads seed in all directions.

Different Wheels

Some wheels are small. Skateboards and scooters race down the street. Tractors have smaller front wheels. This lets the tractor turn more easily. In the back, the big wheels handle most of the work.

Cars used for drag racing have small front wheels and large back wheels.

Other wheels are huge. Some wheels measure more than 13 feet (4 meters). They weigh more than 11 thousand pounds (4,989 kilograms). These wheels go on a dump truck. Other trucks have several wheels. How many axles would go with an 18-wheeler?

A tire bigger than you? Yes! Check out this haul truck.

Wheels can be unusual. A trundle wheel measures distance. How does it work? You push the wheel. It clicks every meter. Count the clicks. Now you know the distance. Fifty clicks equals 50 meters.

Wheels can transport you in different ways. A Ferris wheel will take you high in the sky. Lower to the ground is a Cyr wheel. It stands a little taller than you. Place your hands above and feet below on the wheel. Now you can roll!

Daniel Cyr, a circus performer, is the inventor of the Cyr wheel.

Simple machines save effort. They make work easier. The wheel and axle is ready to roll for your next hard task.

Activity: Build a Car

You can make a car with a few materials. You'll be rolling in no time. An adult will need to help you.

Supplies
- two barbecue skewers
- four bottle caps
- four CDs or DVDs
- drill
- hot glue gun
- paper towel roll

Directions
1. Have an adult help you drill a hole in the center of each bottle cap.

2. Glue the rim of a cap on the outside of a CD or DVD. Do this for all four.

3. Place a barbecue skewer through the front of the paper towel roll. Do the same through the back of the roll.

4. Place a CD on each end of a barbecue skewer. Now you have a car!

GLOSSARY

axle (AK-suhl): a rod in the center of a wheel, around which the wheel turns

complex (KAHM-pleks): having a large number of parts

effort (EF-urt): the activity of trying hard to achieve something

force (fors): any action that produces, stops, or changes the shape or the movement of an object

friction (FRIK-shuhn): the force that slows down objects when they rub against each other

tiller (TIL-ur): a machine that prepares land for growing crops

Using a wheel and axle makes light work of lifting a heavy load! The effort **force** is smaller than the load force.

INDEX

SHOW WHAT YOU KNOW

1. What are the six simple machines?

2. Name two items at school that use wheels.

3. Name two items at home that use wheels.

4. What is the purpose of a trundle wheel?

5. What is the purpose of an axle?

FURTHER READING

Barger, Jeff, *How to Build Box Cars and Trucks*, Rourke Educational Media, 2018.

Doudna, Kelly, *The Kids' Book of Simple Machines: Cool Projects & Activities that Make Science Fun!*, Mighty Media Kids, 2015.

Yasuda, Anita, *Explore Simple Machines!: With 25 Great Projects (Explore Your World)*, Nomad Press, 2011.

ABOUT THE AUTHOR

Jeff Barger is an author, blogger, and literacy specialist. He lives in North Carolina. You will not see him in a Cyr wheel anytime soon.

Meet The Author!
www.meetREMauthors.com

www.rourkeeducationalmedia.com

PHOTO CREDITS: Cover and Title Pg ©Jared Skarda; Pg 3, 5, 7, 8, 11, 16, 18, 20, 24 ©lolon; Pg 5, 6, 9, 11, 12, 15, 16, ©eriksvoboda; Pg 1, 3, 4, 5, 6, 7, 8, 9, 10, 11, 12, 13, 14, 15, 16, 17, 18, 19, 20, 21, 22, 23, 24 ©Amtitus; Pg 4 ©benedek; Pg 5 ©andresr; Pg 6 ©Bill_Vorasate; Pg 7 ©Nerthuz, ©choicegraphx, ©S847; Pg 8 ©krblokhin, Pg 9 ©HomePixel; Pg 10 ©fcafotodigital; Pg 11 ©asiseeit; Pg 12 ©By Leah-Anne Thompson; Pg 13 ©Steve Debenport; Pg 14 ©Ljupco; Pg 15 ©pepifoto; Pg 16 ©dan_prat; Pg 17 ©Leit_Wolf, Pg 18 ©BartCo; Pg 19 ©By Dmitrijs Bindemanis; Pg 20 ©LuckyBusiness, ©Chalabala; Pg 21 ©rambo182, ©nongnewnun12; Pg 22 ©vau902

Edited by: Keli Sipperley
Cover and interior design by: Rhea Magaro-Wallace

Library of Congress PCN Data

Wheel and Axle / Jeff Barger
(Simple Machines)
ISBN 978-1-64369-040-7 (hard cover)
ISBN 978-1-64369-098-8 (soft cover)
ISBN 978-1-64369-187-9 (e-Book)
Library of Congress Control Number: 2018956025

Rourke Educational Media
Printed in the United States of America
01-3472111937